THE RUN OF THE HOUSE

*Johns Hopkins: Poetry and Fiction*

*John T. Irwin, General Editor*

# The Run of the House

WYATT PRUNTY

The Johns Hopkins University Press
Baltimore and London

This book has been brought to publication with the generous assistance of the Albert Dowling Trust.


Printed in the United States of America on acid-free paper

The Johns Hopkins University Press
2715 North Charles Street
Baltimore, Maryland 21218-4319
The Johns Hopkins Press Ltd., London

LIBRARY OF CONGRESS CATALOGING-IN-PUBLICATION DATA

Prunty, Wyatt.
The run of the house : poems / by Wyatt Prunty.
p. cm. — (Johns Hopkins, poetry and fiction)
ISBN 0-8018-4625-0 (acid-free paper). — ISBN 0-8018-4626-9 (pbk.: acid-free paper)
I. Title. II. Series.
PS3566.R84R86 1993
811'.54—dc20 92-43034

A catalog record for this book is available from the British Library.

Some poems in this volume appeared, some in slightly different form, in the following periodicals: "A Note of Thanks," *American Scholar*; "The Elbow Tree," "Haying," and "The Offset," *The Bread Loaf Anthology*; "Cousins, Brothers, Sisters," *New Criterion*; "Elderly Lady Crossing on Green," *Formalist*; "The Angel and the Beast," *New England Review*; "Cold Watercolor," published as "After the Wars," *New Virginia Review*; "Blue Miniatures," *Pacific Review*; "Blood" and "Flying at Night," *Sewanee Review*; "The Taking Down," *Sewanee Theological Review*; "The Inventor," *Shenandoah*; "Baseball," "Distances," "Haying," and "The Water Slide along the Beach," *Southern Review*; and "A Box of Leaves," *Verse*.

FOR BARBARA

CONTENTS

# 1

# HAYING

They are gathering hay. The truck rolls slowly.
The men walk on either side, lifting bales,
Talking without looking up. When one truck fills
Another takes its place, the loaded truck
Turning for the barn, where another crew waits
To get the bales up to the loft.
                                        There is a boy
They've hired for one day; he gets half wages.
They've put him at the top where it's hot,
Where he drags the bales from the lazy belt.
He can't lift the bales, so he backs then tugs,
Backs then tugs, feeling the barn's tin roof bake down.

They've worked since 6 A.M. and now the sun
Enlarges through the trees, which line the field's
Far edge, where the other crew follows a truck.
The older men wear overalls; the young men
Are stripped to the waist. The boy still wears his shirt.
Twice he has tried tobacco, twice gotten sick,
But now he is tired and elated,
Seeing the field's last load turning towards the barn.

Then tugging a bale, he brushes the nest.
And there are yellow jackets everywhere.
And the stings are everywhere, under his shirt,
On his ears, down each arm, and he is running,
Tripping, stung, running again, stung, climbing
Through the stings and rolling along the loft,
Another sting, and the loft's floor opening

And he sees the battered truck, the men circled
And he is on the truck's bed looking up,
The men still circled, and gazing down.
They don't move him, they will not move him,
And he can't move himself.
                                        Old Smythe bends near
And puts tobacco on the stings.
He breaks a cigarette, chews the tobacco,
Then puts it on a sting—here, there, another . . .
Then another cigarette.
                                    He asks the boy
Can he move his legs. The boy says, no,
Yes, maybe . . . maybe in a minute.

The men talk on, as calmly as before—
Complain about the heat, swat flies, light up.
The doctor's on his way and it's all right
Because they meant to quit, needed to,
Else they would have started the next field
And never gotten home.
                                    Lie there, boy,
And listen to their neutral voices—
Used for selecting seed, planting, calving,
Used when ringing necks or cutting calves to steers,
Used for harvest, slaughter, funerals, drought—
And August always turns to drought,
One baking gust that cures the grass
Like a breath inhaled and held
So long that light turns colors.

## THE FERRIS WHEEL

The rounding steeps and jostles were one thing;
And he held tight with so much circling.
The pancaked earth came magnifying up,
Then shrank, as climbing backward to the top
He looked ahead for something in the fields
To stabilize the wheel.

Sometimes it stopped. The chairs rocked back and forth,
As couples holding hands got off
And others climbed into the empty chairs;
Then they were turning, singles, pairs,
Rising, falling through everything they saw,
Whatever thing they saw.

Below—the crowd, a holiday of shirts,
Straw hats, balloons, and brightly colored skirts,
So beautiful, he thought, looking down now,
While the stubborn wheel ground on, as to allow
Some stark monotony within,
For those festooned along the rim.

The engine, axle, spokes, and gears were rigged
So at the top the chairs danced tipsy jigs,
A teetering both balanced and extreme,
"Oh no," the couples cried, laughing, "Stop!" they screamed
Over the rounding down they rode along,
Centrifugal and holding on.

And he held too, thinking maybe happiness
Was simply going on, kept up unless
The wheel slowed or stopped for good. Otherwise,
There were the voices, expectant of surprise;
Funny to hear, he thought, their cries, always late,
Each time the wheel would hesitate,

Since the genius of the wheel was accident,
The always-almost that hadn't,
A minor agony rehearsed as fun
While the lights came up and dark replaced the sun,
Seeming to complete their going round all day,
Paying to be turned that way.

Later, standing off, he felt the wheel's mild dread,
Going as though it lapped the miles ahead
And rolled them up into the cloudless black,
While those who rode accelerated back
And up into the night's steep zero-G
That proved them free.

## THE ELBOW TREE

A sapling bent and tied to point the way,
First, it looked deformed, then got another look,
From getting read by all the tribes who followed.
The rigid elbow, locked till almost freakish,
Could make a match for any highway sign,
Except each year the bending stretched a bit . . .
Until in time the posture grew extreme,
With limbs pointing upward to one side,
And the tree still signing silently,
“This way, and you will not be lost.”

Thus seen thus understood, and nothing changed
What the tree became, nothing altered
What the living figure grew to mean
To those who knew the way and bent the tree
And those who read the figure and followed,
While the trunk and limbs increased with age,
Knotting in potency above the seeds
That fell countless and unaccountable
In blinding freedom from the tree that was
In one thing bent and in another made.

## THE MONUMENT

Standing apart yet oddly sequential
In our timed and untimed arrivals, some
Casually late, some impatiently prompt,
But indeed all lining up respectfully,
Just as the signs have said we ought to do,
We watch the elevator dial start up then stop
Then start again, sweeping along its scale
As off ahead near where the line begins
A mother reads aloud from a guidebook
To her children, who yawn and do not listen . . .

As the pulleys to the elevator drone,
Spinning down through the shaft that takes us up,
Till the ornate arrow slows and settles
Over the double doors' subtractive whoosh
And lets the crowd that's gone before step off
And shoulder by without a single hint
Why we should take their place, shouldering up,
As now it's our time on the steep ascent,
Where we will push then pause then crowd us through,
Not seeing the symbol but the view.

## THE INVENTOR

You had to have power, he knew that,
So the engine went rattling up front—
And the wings, delicate as Jacob's limp,
"The wings were definitive," he'd say.
And then the lesser facts for lifting off . . .
The thorax shape in which he sat,
And, tightened aft, two modest surfaces
For the ups and downs, each right or left.
There were the struts, turn-buckled wires, deft pulleys,
All angling so many little tensions
And whistling as the wind picked up.
In fact he couldn't count the symphony he'd built,
Though many things were left out, that first time.
But he got a buck and glide alright,
Then yawed the whole damn thing, catching two trees
As the wings hit evenly and sheared.

The wings could be replaced. He wasn't hurt.
He knew the secret, thrust and lift,
Venturi's insight cut in half;
Lift came out of a lessening,
The wings' curve speeding, thinning the air—
Until going up was, briefly, the easier choice.
So up he went, this first time . . . and down too,
Clipping his moth-like wings between two oaks.

While he waited for Bertie, Betty, and Louis,
For Simone, the terrestrial mechanic,
His little thorax held him upside down,
Smiling in the certainty that this was a thing,
Like so many other things these days,
To be built en masse, and with no reverse.

## INDUCED LIGHT

From the complex brightening of chandeliers
Beneath which the general and the diplomat
Lean together in an exchange of names
Then walk off to the indirect light
Of an alcove where no one will overhear . . .
Or from the floodlights sweeping down the lawn
To widen where the walkways end
And leave us gazing into their patterns
Repeating in circular green after green
The illusion of their power over green . . .
And from the softer lights we place about
As if their circles were rounded from within
Instead of circumscribed by where they fade . . .
From these, and all the other lights we see,
And generate, and by which we say we see—
To the shaded, single, light bulb overhead
That rakes one face and hides another . . .
Is the distance of the ordinary wires
That the ordinary workmen put in walls,
Which, insulated, buried even,
In the deep masonry of foundations
Are serviceable every night for as long
As anyone wanting them may leave them on.

Meanwhile, the business underneath one bulb
Goes on as starkly visible as ever,
Where the colonnade leads to the concrete slab
On which kneels the soldier or civilian
Already broken, or soon to be broken,
By what the man behind the shade has learned
About one pain's power over another—
That animals in traps chew off their parts,
Chew off a leg or paw to hobble free.

The questioning goes on, long after dark,
Long past the crisp reception's close,
While the general sleeps or sits awake
Smoking in the dark, rehearsing all the moves,
The chessboard moves whose rules require
Opposing players, mirrored openings,
To which the diplomat himself will step,
While elsewhere someone kneels, giving answers,
Wrong or desperately true, and in a place
That no opposing figure will confirm.

## DECEMBER LIGHT

Seen through a haze that shallows everything,
Streetlights, the early kitchens, a neighbor's car
Pausing before it turns out from its drive—
The day begins, B-grade and black and white,
As one dog barks, then another in return,
And blocks away a siren climbs into pitch
Then dwindles with distance to a fire,
Or false alarm, or early heart attack;
And the haze, still brighter now, fills in
With houses, grown from solitary lights
Into the rare dimensions of their rooms,
The way a miner's darkness shells his lamp
And where he walks are provinces resumed
From the lignite and bituminous damp
Of what he did not mine the day before
But left ahead, marking another start.

We could use nothing in December more
Than leaving some unfinished part,
As we fall past sleep into another day
Where we will finish something left undone
The day before, when we felt the dark delay
Toward night crowding and shouldering down
Into our houses . . . as now stunned mornings follow
And what was once the tenth month of the year
Goes beneath a sun from which nothing grows
Except our shadows, which stretch and disappear.

## OPENING THE MIRROR

Loosen the frame and slide the glass
Past where you see yourself and do not move,
Until you see behind your looking back;

Night cities barge out through the frame,
Tunneling in their blues and greens,
Then reds that deepen and disappear.

Count the skylines drifting out of sight
Like slow freights headed through a point
That is the eye's blind spot and aperture;

Follow the way fixed landscapes slide,
Sluing at first then sideways gone
Out of the frame's bland vacancy,

Leaving behind the smoke and dust
Of streets, highways, and tracks curling
Like celluloid through the frame,

Where thin lines weave in helices
That join sometimes and sometimes break
But go their way anyway, twisting from sight.

Open the hidden forwarding light;
Stand where the frame becomes the shaft
Of what the mirror stood before . . .

As if before the unreflected light
Of a theater with the screen let down
Whose heros and heroines wave

Forever ahead of that point
Where those who pay to see will ever see
Because the long light from before

Tunnels through the blue smoke overhead,
And neither nouns nor caves will bury it back,
Now that the mirror does not stand for you.

## AND ONLY AFTER

Pigeon-toed, those skates on stairs,
Guests descending unaware;
For it's high-ho, and ha, and hee,
And off with everybody.

A quiet grief, a quiet house;
Its halls and rooms cavernous
Without the dangerous stairs
Where laughter gears,

Demanding every answer
Questioned, demanding fear
Of a sort be set aside
By what I can't provide

So only say—the fueling no
Of now, and now you know.

## STILLNESS

Returning to the spent house its emptiness,
Letting its windows go as they have gone,
Opened from one abandonment to another,
To the yard grown wildly immeasurable
In the greens, reds, yellows, and browns
Of a fall that comes like someone pausing
Between remembering a name and speaking
The long recollection that a name unfolds . . .

Or, leaving the sagging doors ajar,
Stuck in disagreement with their hinges
And forever met halfway between
Closing on those who left for good
And opening to the abandoned, useless
Ways our going away made of them . . .

Returning to these stubborn, collapsing facts
That are not themselves but always us,
The ones who took their meals and slept upstairs,
There where no stairs can lead us now,
There where the quiet things said before sleep
Are forever truly quiet . . . returning
As if to someone else's carefulness,
We now take down by board and nail
All we ever loved and drove into place.

## THE WEDDING STOP

The walls were thin, and when he left
To dig out something in the trunk
She heard the TV from one side,
While on the other voices rose—
Children complaining, someone explaining.

Later, she watched her husband's face relax
Into a loosened version of himself,
Slack jaw against one arm, face turned,
As where he slept he deepened alone.
So she let the day replay itself,
The white of her continuous day,
With its music, smiles, and flowers.

And then there was the white-noise fan
Loud in the vent above her head
And the intervals of something like crying,
Till she thought about her parents' house,
The outside cold lengthening their hall . . .
There was the crying somewhere, the fan,
Her husband's breathing. Then she slept.

In the morning, loud pipes and voices,
So she eased out, palms cautioning the door,
Where she stepped backwards, watching her husband sleep.
Then she was by herself and got a look . . .
A woman off a ways, shadowed in her door,
Drawn mouth, three children standing back of her.
Then all of them were in their jumbled car,
With its smeared windows and fitful engine,
Till the balding man behind the wheel
Found reverse, and the car lurched backwards
Through its blue exhaust. And still she was glad.

## ELDERLY LADY CROSSING ON GREEN

And give her no scouts doing their one good deed
Or sentimental cards to wish her well
During Christmas time or gallstone time—
Because there was a time, she'd like to tell,

She drove a loaded V8 powerglide
And would have run you flat as paint
To make the light before it turned on her,
Make it as she watched you faint

When looking up you saw her bearing down
Eyes locking you between the wheel and dash,
And you either scrambled back where you belonged
Or jaywalked to eternity, blown out like trash

Behind the grease spot where she braked on you. . . .
Never widow, wife, mother, or a bride,
And nothing up ahead she's looking for
But asphalt, the dotted line, the other side,

The way she's done a million times before,
With nothing in her brief to tell you more
Than she's a small tug on the tidal swell
Of her own sustaining notion that she's doing well.

## A BOX OF LEAVES

Collected from childhood's high October,
And sealed under the milky paraffin
Almost forever as they were,
These reds, browns, and yellows, not of a season
But of a season's end, are our reminders
Of a simplicity we never tire
Of telling: that we are lost among ourselves;
Like Dante's suicides, the slightest gust
Tears us from our proper stems to scuttle
In a crowd of bent and drying ironies.
We say no two are ever quite the same
Yet never see that two as different,
Except, perhaps, in how, having lasted
For a long time, such category
May loosen grip, widening from sight.
"Leaves," we say, and generalize each leaf away
In a summary of qualities
Changeable as a season's changing weather.
Waxed, labeled, and carefully put from sight,
These wait alone, safely past their calendar;
Frail and familiar, foreign and lovely,
Not as themselves but as their others.

## THE WATER SLIDE ALONG THE BEACH

It is someone's mimicry, the clockworks
Of wave and tide and shifting weather,
Which, when filled and turned on, makes rhythmical
The textured and turquoised edge of our stilled gulf.

Ages ten and seven, they beg to go.
And so we take them, swayed backs, taut bellies
Poking forward like impudence.
They are brown enough to be ripe or cooked . . .

*And symmetrical as the conchs they find,*
*Always with the same exclamations,*
*The small empty shells they see as beautiful*
*Because they echo the one who listens.*

*It is the blood's clichéd continuum,*
*Traveling from ear to shell to ear again,*
*That reassures them of their small full seas,*
*The long grays and blues that wait ahead for them,*

*The tides that will rise for their departures*
*Or that will drop, leaving their hulls mired and leaning . . .*
*And promised vessels passing out of sight*
*Topping the horizon, where, briefly magnified,*

*They disappear beyond the wavy plane*
*Of humane endurance, in which we think*
*The gulls cry with almost human voices,*
*Think the stark similes of looking out.*

*The ships depart. Flags fade. The ships go down,*
*Down the round that even children know about,*
*Where China is not reached by pick or shovel,*
*Only where the lens quits and the eye blinks shut.*

Now our nut-brown pair is at the top.
They are waving. We wave encouragement.
Racing down, they bounce, spin, and scream laughter.
Helped out, their wet hands leave wide prints; they drip,

Wipe noses, rush off, demanding that we watch. . . .
As if those most powerful ever
Let us drop our eyes from where they see us
Magnified, topping their horizons.

# 2

## BLOOD

Known for its repertory lineages
By which we generalize the who and what,
And for the figures that we make of it,
Bloodline, bloodlust . . . it runs between
The spent asphyxiated blues
Of time and work and that bright filigree
Through which the impounding heart pumps back
Our reddened and ventilated lives—
As if among the wind's announcing leaves
That dryly say the world's deciduous,
We breathed a lasting shape that let us stay.

Scripted in a secret and minute hand
That writes itself and signs its origins
In unrepeated blues and reds,
The blood holds to its systole and diastole,
Flooding and circling rawly on
As rhythmic tides reduplicate their shores,
As opened wounds edge inward, welling,
Fresh surfacing and taken by the air . . .
Till drying to a lake-bed crust of drought,
There where the healing scab prevents the scar,
Blood surfaces our dust, and something more,
The potent changing earth of us.

## A NOTE OF THANKS

Wallet stolen, so we must end our stay.
Then, while checking out, the wallet reappears
With an unsigned note saying, "Please forgive me;
This is an illness I have fought for years,
And for which you've suffered innocently.
P.S. I hope you haven't phoned about the cards."
I wave the wallet so my wife will see.
Smiling, she hangs up, and smiling she regards
The broad array of others passing by,
Each now special and uniquely understood.
We go back to our unmade room and laugh,
Happily agreeing that the names for "good"
Are not quite adequate and that each combines
Superlatives we but rarely think.
For the next three nights we drink a better wine.
And everyday we go back through to check
The shops, buying what before had cost too much,
As if now Christmas and birthdays were planned
Years in advance. We watch others and are touched
To see how their faces are a dead-panned
Generality, holding close
The wishes and desires by which we all are gripped.
All charities seem practical to us,
All waiters deserving of a bigger tip.
And, though we counter such an urge,
We start to think we'd like to meet the thief,
To shake the hand of self-reforming courage
That somehow censored a former disbelief.

Then we are home and leafing through the bills
Sent us from an unknown world of pleasure;
One of us likes cheap perfume; the other thrills
Over shoes, fedoras, expensive dinners;
There are massage parlors and videos,
Magazines, sunglasses, pharmaceuticals,
Long-distance calls, a host of curios,
Gallons of booze. . . . Only now we make our call.
But then, on hold, we go on sifting through
The mail till turning up a postcard view
Of our hotel. Flipping it and drawing blanks,
We read, "So much enjoyed my stay with you
I thought I ought to jot a note of thanks."

## BASEBALL

About the time I got my first baseman's mitt
I heard that Dizzy Dean was sacked
Because he made a dirty comment
Over the air. Camera zoomed and locked
On a young couple kissing, something slipped
With Dizzy, who then made the call:
"He kisses her on every strike,
And she kisses him on the balls."

In a century banked with guilt and doubt
Sometimes the telling moments come
As inadvertently as Dizzy's joke,
Like Hitler's code before Coventry was bombed,
Or Valéry's remark about Descartes,
"I sometimes think, therefore I sometimes am."

## ANOTHER SCARECROW

Clichéd particulars, the sticks, straw, old clothes.
At least it's got a fixed perspective,
Hung up and looking west over the corn
With a constancy we only imagine.

Small children frighten, then have to touch.
But what they really fear they do not see . . .
That the crossed sticks beneath the coat might hold
More than the blank face, sad hat, and sagging sleeves.

Lashed together with some wrapping twine,
The whole thing puts the farmer out among his rows
All over again, but that the coat's
Got parts covered so you cannot tell.

Say the scarecrow's no more hung from his frame
Than held up by it. Say it is his skeleton,
Which long after the clothes are blown from sight,
Sometime in a January snow,

Will jut darkly up the capital *T*
Of an uncompleted word, whose genius
Was that when we clothed it as ourselves
It made a shadow and drove the birds away.

## FLYING AT NIGHT

Each city is a solitary reef,
Brightening under a phosphorescent tide
At once astringent and invisible.
Lights pulse their distances in strings,
Either purling out to a wider dark
Or squaring a downtown's grid to imitate
The world's steep longitudes, its latitudes.
Sometimes a single car glides down a street,
Its headlights' two white cones tunneling,
And only lighting where the driver has
Already turned. How strange it is to see
The empowered light following that way.
Suddenly the radio erupts
With weather, times, and late advisories.
A voice enumerates; the engine drones.

Then you are out of range for radios
And following an arbitrary line
Across a landscape with its unplanned lights
By which no one can navigate and where
The darkest ridges rise invisibly. . . .
And should the engine stop, there is this joke:
You cannot tell which dark beneath will be
A forest, ridge, or field, so just before
You're down, cut on the landing light,
Then if you don't like what you see, cut it off.
There is that joke . . . which only gets
It's laughter in daylight and on the ground.

For now, the small plane's red interior
Of night lights, maps, and instruments
Powers through two kinds of dark—cities
That sometimes wake and sometimes are asleep,
And overhead an older population,
Orion, Andromeda, Perseus . . .
Who with their dippers, the lion, bull, and fish
Arrange our darkened ways for out and back,
Most accurately and uncaringly so,
As sometimes to one side the local moon
Pulls up and pales us with its used light,
Under which we go, plying our lost and found.

## LETTER FOR THE END *for Howard Nemerov*

Who would want to become his admirers?
Still, he was so gracious at the end
It was our sorrow that he talked away
In his genial Job-like manner.

For years he cataloged our likenesses,
Through the leaf-spent acids of seasons
Raked and burned or rotting implosively,
Their figures turned like witnesses

To a proof inside the indelible
Cold, tightening each fall toward winter.
And then there were the snows, whose white chaos
Was as pure as unintelligible,

For the sleepless boy, or the waking man
Discovering once more he only watched
The beautiful despairing joke repeat . . .
Where raked leaves ever took their trees again.

Anything to say to make things better,
Of how the random seeds inscribed their end
By dying upward into power.
Knowing this, for years he wrote his letter.

## THE BALLOONS

Their softened surfaces turn crowfeet now,
As touched they sink further, here where
Before we filled them and let them go
And let our following eyes bob after

Nearly in time to the music playing,
As they scuttled up to float beyond
Their first depth, languidly rising
Side to side and bladdering overhead,

At once bunched, eddying, and passive . . .
Till halted at their local height, they bumped
From side to side where the ceiling planed their rise,
Leveling the lightness that had brought them up.

Later, still bright amid the shuffled party,
They left their heights to tap us on our shoulders,
As if along the eye's periphery
Shy drunks were breaking for our partners.

Then gassed out and failing inwardly,
They lingered in a stalled midair
Of incomplete gestures, plump symmetries
Softening inevitably down to where

The hardwood floor became a shelf,
Shouldering what before the ceiling held
Of their clambering up . . . these shrunken selves,
Sinking in their wrinkled greens, blues, and reds.

## GOING ON

Some accidents exist ahead of time . . .
The balance artist's faulty props,
That shaky ladder, and the limb cut through;

And then there are those dings, dents, or benders
In parking lots graphed for minor incidents
To which the traffic rules do not apply,

Also the serial bumps down corridors
And elevator doors that do not wait,
And then a staircase telescoping underfoot.

Driving, sometimes you imagine what's ahead,
Beyond the dips, rises, and blind curves . . .
Until your own inverted wheels are spinning.

Today you go your ordinary way,
The January sun low on your left,
Which means you're driving north, for now,

Though soon you'll turn directly to the sun,
Heading toward home, the radio fading
And you squinting in the rapid light

The low sun telegraphs from trees
Like static on the radio,
While the engine hums its monotone.

In June, the same turn west means shade.
But today, the trees shade nothing;
They only tighten in their dormant ranks.

Sometimes a sign divides them like a promise,
But the trees close back, they always close;
And where you look you hear the light break up.

## THE BACKWARD LOOK

Driving away, on the road that runs away
And runs back home, you sometimes look
Out of a half-collected turn of thought
That causes you to crook your neck,
Gazing back for what it is you leave,
As feeling yourself moving both off and on,
You either straighten your head and disappear
Through what you see, or find you cannot turn;
And though the car continues ahead,
Geared and combustible, rattling out smoke,
You lose yourself, there, in the backward look,

Which serves for brave send-offs at the pier,
Great arm waves from the ladder to the plane,
And all the rest manners allow
To speed you through the terminal toward claims . . .
And still the backward look, persistent and clear,
Reversing every way you go,
Like the negative to something bright,
The nothing in the mirror's left and right.

# COLD WATERCOLOR

We saw the birds jockeying for the feeder.
Inside, the networks fed us New Year's Day.
And then there was the snow, in thick raw blots
Down past a row of windows where it caught,
Turning the sills to ridges, as outside
The streets, houses, and yards thickened
From their named and numbered ways into
A watercolor unreadably white . . .
And all the while the manic snow descending,
Sometimes glazed against a pane but mostly
Falling from itself into itself
Under a low, bruised, and indefinite sky. . . .

Until the things I watched to measure change,
A recent stump, raised flower beds, porch steps—
Had disappeared, with the snow still falling
And the gray January light fading,
Fusing the trees and houses in one shade . . .
Suddenly a shadow now, beyond the glass
That mirrored us with looking out,
Ourselves out there, watches and rings reversed—
As reporters had the years reversed,
We said, looking out, seeing us looking in.

Later, the snow stopped and clouds cleared,
Our local ceiling shrank to absolute.
Standing outside, we swayed with gazing up,
Swayed because the stars were high and deep,
How odd that something overhead was deep,
And still the snow's thick watercolor white.
And then there were the brisk good-byes—
Closing an afternoon and evening spent
In the snow's knee-deep and numberless house,
Where, the usual wishes being said,
The door left standing wide, its angled light
Fanning the stalled abandoned plow,
We let the buried street run on ahead,
As following our shadows from the porch,
We stepped out of the light into our whitened way.

## OLD DECLARATIVES

No calculation holds the miles endured.
Perhaps that's why some families seem stunned,
Waiting in stations or out by tracks,
Patting their pockets to check for tickets,
Their small clasped bags almost identical . . .
As are the ways they have paid, paid the same
Fare to the same repeating agent,
Then pressed themselves in bunches through drawn doors,
Reading the smudged signs identifying seats
Where, adjusting and looking ahead
Or back, they nod, and sometimes sleep. . . .

Outside, the fields drift by like a promise,
To the immigrant believing seasons change
Predictably, that what he plants will rise
In fairness to the hours he has worked.
And next, the landscape interrupts itself.
No one knew the towns could grow so tired.
The chimneys are silent flutes; each window's *X*'d.
Walking off the job, thousands must have stumped
Through the sludge, junk and the bent, sighing grass
Where the tracks, however parallel,
Narrowed the same way either way.

Were there a guidebook, it would say
To take another route; it would advise
A trip into the mountains where the view
Adjusts itself, where trees have overgrown
The mine shaft's rails and the tunnel's dark descent.
Or else it would suggest the ocean's gray
Reflexive tides that wash their limits up
From underneath, where limits never held.
And in that same guidebook, perhaps there is
A page torn out, some missing numbers
That will never say what slips past now . . .

Empty streets, dead yards and tumbled houses,
The blank windows of red brick factories
Where some once marched or were let go.
And other replicas that become us—
A small girl's doll, weed-sunken swings,
The way the closed hotel's cracked masonry
Confirms its long abandonment . . .
Or, here, now, suddenly a low salt marsh
That duplicates the reddening sky,
Where three mute gulls have landed for the night
And step together, step darkly red together.

# 3

## COUSINS, BROTHERS, SISTERS

When I was five and said I'd seen an angel,
They said it was the Phantom waiting for me
Because I rivaled him in ugliness.
Jealous, he was hiding in the angle

Of the shadow of my bedroom door;
Or he was standing in the upstairs hall,
Patient, silent, and invisible
To anyone he was waiting for.

That summer every night was filled with losses.
When I was sent upstairs alone to bed,
I stared on vacancies—long shadowed halls
With doors ajar, dark windows, distant voices.

Now that I've seen death's ugliness,
Dyeing us in the many shades he takes,
I know I watched in awe, that sleep came on
From dark to darker emptiness,

While the voices down the stairs or up the hall
Talked on awhile, then paused, then stopped,
As the others too took their darkened beds
And the house unfolded upward from us all.

## LIGHTNING

Walking the bluff above the town,
I watched the lightning working west to east.
At first it traveled cloud to cloud,
Its bunkered thunder echoing miles
Between the flash and clap.

I counted, figuring distances,
Watching the storm making its way.
And then there was the wind, brief, strong,
And the lightning forking down across the fields
Like a bright inverted branch;

Then it was striking up instead of down,
Once, twice, again, and the thunder following
Each ragged, strobe-like reach of light
That fingered out, spastic and skeletal,
Dividing the dark,

Until another gust, the smell of rain,
Roll cloud and anvil overhead,
And the rain down through the trees, deafening
Down through the trees, which twisted in the wind,
Leaves tearing in the wind,

Each flash—the trees, another flash,
As the lightning came on, streaking down,
Painting the valley and town below
Where the lights were out and everything
Was drawn in miniature

And bright, in the afterimage of the eye.
And then another strike, bleaching the town,
Magnifying all it touched, until
Its tentacles and spiders' legs
Walked the daylight valley into dark.

## DISTANCES

Six horses painted red and blue and anchored
To concrete slabs. Six children climb and mount.
The horses sway on springs that are coil and leaf,
Each capable of its own crazy gait,
In which no movement ever quite repeats.

The children ride, leaning forward and back,
Tipping their heads as if they drank and swallowed
With exaggerated ahs, while underneath
The springs tighten and bend, first rhythmically
Then separately, as the horses gather speed.

Mostly the children lunge and look ahead,
Focused on some midair object we can't see.
Riding, they nod; and the horses nod
Blankly, underneath, as each one goes on
Alone on its path of ruts and rises.

And that is what the children make believe.
They are alone. The horses do not stay
But pitch miles forward, sometimes slowing,
When their riders hold them carefully,
Then going on, in a flexed monotony.

The parents are missing. There are no parents.
Someone has let the children off. Books, coats,
A pair of skates are left along the ground
As though dropped while running to the horses.
These make a jagged line across the grass.

It is growing dark, but no one comes to take
The children home. Shadows arrive, dissolve.
Still no one comes. If someone did, the children
Would not turn or answer. Now the light recedes,
But nothing changes. And the horses tip and lunge.

## MISS LUCY

First day each fall she lectured
On William of Ockham—who he was,
How wrong he was . . . and always would remain.
Then, warning they'd never understand,
She made them memorize Augustine's lines,
Each of them embarrassed to recite—that
"They begin to depart who begin to love.
Many there are who depart without knowing it."

For the betterment of style, there were
Shakespeare's kings, Lycidas, and Wordsworth's Lucy,
Then the Prayer of Humble Access, which she scrawled
Across the board and made them copy,
"We do not presume," they all scrawled back . . .
Till they copied, cribbed, dozed, skipped, and muddled
Through their year with her, their senior year,
As she reminded them, all year.

They'd seen her clothes in black and white movies.
That much they knew, that and her shoes
Looked like miniature pilings. Shadowing
The hall ahead, she marched, arms counterpoised,
As though she'd joined the Royal Navy.
Six feet, high forehead, thin hair on top,
She had a man's falsetto voice by which
All points of view were torqued third person.

“Now class, she once began, Miss Lucy
Cannot be with you for the game tonight;
You’ll have to ride your busses there and back
Without her. Remember who you are,
As Miss Lucy will have you in mind.
She will be stationed by her radio
Monitoring your game. Miss Lucy is
A strong athletic supporter.”

That time they laughed out loud,
Though years later what they recalled
Was not the game’s score but how her eyes
Scanned back and forth, slicing the room,
Before she asked them what “saccadic” meant,
Then wrote it on the board, scanned them again
And, turning from their reddened hush, printed
“Scotoma.” Did they know what the word meant?

## GREAT THOUGHTS AND NOBLE FEELINGS

A storm, and our window frames the ocean
Like a fluid Turner down the wall.
The waves kick up in a horrible fit
That really would elevate, if someone read

Aloud something Gothic and about graveyards.
And each ecstatic wave's a dying beauty
Splayed out on the sand and bubbling
Better than Lizzie Siddal as Ophelia.

For in between, there's drink, with which we stretch out
Under the long twilight the clouds impose,
Like some great brooding revelation, stalled
Above the daily grind and bubble.

Linked backward to the shore by telephone,
Cable, the mail, newspapers, magazines,
We look into the rich and recondite
Storm, but think our condominium.

This is what the masters meant to teach us,
A sovereignty of sorts, somewhere between
What the decorator's done to everyday,
Inside the atelier we vacuum up,

And what the storm outside does by itself;
Though the spark leap, the longing rise like dough,
We know we are alone, where the ocean's wide
Periphery teaches our narrow passage.

## THE ENDEAVOR *5/13/92*

As though going out improved the light,
Stationed past our moody weather, on site,
As site shrank to coordinates, a sea
Of fixes penciled over vacancies,

And the whole time we were looking out not up,
Though sitting up, with our dark half asleep . . .
As there the three, blandly umbilicus,
Seemed drug-like in their pudgy weightlessness.

They floated before the patched earth's blue and white,
While above, the broken ash-can satellite
Came canted and drifting sideways down
Into a cargo bay that opened on

The other view, the backward sight of us,
Our tocked and tilting earth, we looking back at us.
Castor, Pollux, and a new one without name,
Fetal and albino there along the plane

The lens arranged, were busying on—
Bouncing and bloating up into our down,
Drifting before the pushball earth of us,
Together now, safe-seeming, encompassed

By the lens that way, until the tests
They'd run ran out, and all their busyness
About the bay became the routine shop
Of their Endeavor, long along its slope . . .

As on they worked, the three, speaking easily,
Banking about the bay as precisely
As the backspin shot by which they went
So far away to be no different.

# THE OFFSET

Some miles beyond the last reef's barricade,
Where currents take the local tide to sea
And where, long from the seaward-looking cottage,
The gulls tease, hover and descend, as lightly
As a maple's keys coptering and lost
Over the general waters off this coast,
There the charts agree what's out of range . . .
And there, the practical keel that can't divide
What it crosses divides its way anyway,
Cutting one course from all others, tossed
But steady on the contoured gray.

Just so, because there's any course to take
But only one that's taken right,
And even when it's right then only true
By going off a bit, crabbing its way . . .
As all good pilots learn to do,
Sighting a line that's never without play
And traveling the way the light things go,
Not ahead but spindrift and sideways of sight,
As the imagination does sometimes
To get things right, though seeming to know,
Really off course a bit, but more promising so.

## NEW TERRITORY

Taking a walk on her first retirement day,
She stopped to watch two starlings glinting
As they circled up then down, widened then closed,
Dogfighting some twenty feet above
Around a spot no one else could see;
Spiraling as they rode two helices
Built in the air, as in their heads,
Which hammered whenever they came close.
Then the one knocked the other down,
Made a strafing run, climbed and stalled
Into a wingover and came back down,
Tines out, landing on the wounded bird
And locking his talons on one leg.

She had not moved from where she stopped.
But now the birds were still, except the one
Who held the other cranked his idiot head
Over the wing, broken open like a fan.
Then the one was gone and the broken one left,
Tossed out like a life raft on the grass—
And she deciding what it was she'd do,
Till the chorus rose and bombing runs began,
Starlings out of every corner of the yard
Angling in over the grounded bird,
Beak here and talon there, and blood . . . till she swore
She'd poison the seed then take the feeders down,
As she turned a different way for home.

## CHANGING WEATHER

1

As if the trees disguise themselves,
Turning first a light then darker green,
Until they take October's figured fall
Into the reds and yellows of decay. . . .

No barometric reading means itself.
Numbers high, a cold front bustles in;
Or, from the south, warm air, as now a low
Drifts up, settling grayly for days.

Forecasters poise before new storms
Symboled in their bright geometries;
And there are satellites whose pictures cloud
The future tense, drawn and drifting on the map

In the brief approximations of a herd,
Sometimes distinct but mostly blurred.

2

Meanwhile, there is the rediscovered sky
Of where we wake, which whether blue or gray
Becomes the changes the predictors say,
Or meant to say, early or late . . .

Some systems changed, others dying on their way;
While sleeping or waking to walk and wait
And tolerate the weather that's been said,
We sometimes stop to marvel at

The silent anvil of a thunderhead
Towering into view, as if its fact
Meant something we could read, before
The day goes right or wrong, wet or dry,

As predicted, while watched from below,
The sun said sometimes red, sometimes yellow.

## THE ANGEL AND THE BEAST

Past side streets, cars, and dogs that hesitate . . .
Past curb, drive, or the front yard's difficult gate,
He pilots a circle route home, singing.
Lights follow where his scuffed shoes drum.
On our street, neighbors lift shades and strain
Into the audible dark of their trimmed lots,
As over the hedges and toys left out
Names and the fragment of a song become
Suddenly loud enough for two sound drunks.
Such singing, as though he thought he entertained
Those turning and saying someone should help.

But where he bends as if he had a weight,
Either to throw it off or to raise it,
And where the trees' shadows darken through
His cross-eyed stare, each tree becoming two,
There the hedges hold their lines past light,
And the children's toys range staggered out of sight
In a clutter of forgotten games . . .
And there the half song and the half-heard names
He lists go on as he goes on, stout
And leaning down the street, in the debate
He follows, between the one who tells him slow
And the other who says now.

## ROUND ROBIN

Along the corridor one door's ajar,
And from it there's a shaft of light
That Hopper might have caught, but now the three
Come bumping through, two parents and a child,
The parents signing back and forth,
The boy chatting up beneath their finger talk.
And now the father shakes a fist,
And even I can read what he has said.
Then the mother counters with a rising
Argument that matches the dexterity
Of a surgeon or pianist;
Her fingers go staccato then stop midair,
As if thought stopped beyond her wrist,
Where any moment she might pat or slap her husband.

Meanwhile their son chirps on between them,
Talking to himself and sometimes
Raising a hand also to sign,
Lifting a face to read what they will say.
He follows, separate as his commentary—
They will have dinner now. He is hungry.
Will there be ice cream, can he watch TV?—
There's no reply, as he hurries in place
Between the two above who go along,
First walking down the hall, then turning back.

The boy repeats himself: it's dinner then bed . . .
Although they're off to nowhere he has said,
As they push the two-way finger-spotted doors
That lead outside and lead back in . . .
These silences and their hungry nestling,
Cycling in and out and up and down the hall,
And he conversing upward through it all,

Third person and pleasantly alert,
His voice rising and stoutly resolute . . .
As now they go outside and turn again,
He wheeling where no one explains,
Pivoting under everything they mean,
Whatever they sign, whatever he stands between.

## BLUE MINIATURES

You're driving home alone through neighborhoods
Softened by a drizzle and sinus haze
In which the stoplights sway like pendulums
Each time the wind kicks up, jostling the green
That tells you "yes," the red that argues "no . . . "
When an ambulance slips past, siren rising
As it brisks away, lights working back and forth,
First white then blue, then white then blue
Till it accelerates, brakes, and turns from sight.

The traffic moves, an agreeable herd
That starts and stops in one jugged unison,
Until ahead the ambulance again,
Its lights working their bright monotony
Over a gurney pushed along the walk
By men who look into some vacant point
Above a covered figure on the cot.

Someone has died. Help has come too late.
Or there was no chance, and help came as it could.
The front door to the house is pushed inside,
And the lights are on, and from the street
A kind of doll-house shrinkage gives you leave
To look without emotion on the worst
You know.
                    Meanwhile there's been a life
Of paid particulars, as you realize
The furniture along the walls looks tired
Where the low-watt lighting makes the living room
Seem deeper than it is . . . makes the house seem soft.

Surely you see how soft is, inside,
As in your glassed and insulated weather
You brake and slow and gaze all to one side.
Surely each must feel this is the way we leave . . .
The rest dumbly looking on then looking off,
Accelerating on to their own hard turns
While, legs folding, the gurney slots beneath
The mania the momentary lights kick up.

## THE TAKING DOWN

Ever since the seriously ill were sent away,
The sounds, smells, even the lights have changed;
These days the doctors in the valley
Export their help up to our hospital,
Where rarely anyone walks the corridors,
Now lengthened by their emptiness,
Much the way the parking lots outside
Wait like hugely widened game boards,
Especially during the holidays,
When looking out one thinks of visitors.

After Christmas and before New Year's,
The artificial Christmas tree
Is taken down and packed away
"To avoid bad luck," Mrs. Gilbert says.
She and the other volunteers
Sit in the lobby and quietly pack
The coils of wire that, covered with green needles,
Make up the tree's ten feet of branches.
They put the ornaments in smaller boxes,
Each one sealed, labeled, and numbered
So that, next year, they may reverse themselves.

For Mrs. Gilbert, the emptied corridors
And vacant parking lots mean that her wing
Along the back, looking out into the woods
From its rounded nurses' station, lounge, and rooms,
Has cycled the healing roundabout
Of charts, nurses, and starched doctors
Into something barely graspable—
The indefinite December sky
Under which she walked once as a girl,

Hurrying home and looking side to side
Between the houses' deepening porches,
Until she bundled through her own front door,
Lights out and the hall recessively still.
She remembers sitting alone for hours.

This time of year the drive from the hospital
Stretches as the halls on Mrs. Gilbert's wing
Lengthen in the early dark that seems to stall
The backward counting days before New Year's,
After the Christmas visitors have disappeared;
So Mrs. Gilbert busies herself
A little longer in each room,
And takes some added care in overseeing
That the ornaments and artificial tree
Are packed away by proper count,
Boxes numbered and stacked in sequence,
As though matching next year's calendar
By which she will arrange her hall,
Where she walks now, checking every name,
Steering her cart as she has done for five years.

The back wheels swivel as she moves,
Leaning in a push that makes the cart
Seem heavier than it is. Nothing spills.
And her list of names, which rarely changes,
Is on top, printed new each day for her,
As if she were a silent auditor
Hired to hold some closing inventory.
Sometimes her lips move, naming a new patient.
Other times, she pauses at a vacancy
And checks the room, opening the door
And feeling a draft's subtractive touch.

From down the hall, Mrs. Henry shouts
Repeatedly, "Take Me Home! Take Me Home!"
Then, offered varieties of drink,
Answers softly, "No thank you, Dear, no thank you."
The cart backed out, the shouting starts again.
Next, Mr. Elmo, who's had a stroke:
"I feel so stupid," he says, shaking his head,
"I'm dead because I'm stupid."
She offers him his cup; he looks away.
Later, when she checks, the cup's still full.

Mrs. Nicholas plays the radio all day.
She cannot use her hands to change the station
But doesn't mind, she says, because
She only wants the human voices going on.
Her friend across the hall, Mrs. Austin,
Has lost the use of her two good hands also.
She leans away, then whispers, "Are you a Christian?"
Surprised, Mrs. Gilbert says, "Yes, yes, I am."
"Then would you scratch my nose?"

Next there is Mrs. Alfred, who asks about
Her husband down the hall, "Is he warm enough?"
"It's Alzheimer's, you know." She likes reports
And always sends a note propped by his cup,
Knowing he will fold the note repeatedly,
Tuck it away, take it out, try to read.

Twice now Mrs. Gilbert's wing has telescoped
As though her head were driven back,
Twice the ceiling, walls, and floor contracted
To a half light, then widened and returned,

As she leaned even farther forward
In her exaggerated push against the cart.
Both times her parents came to mind, grown small
In their clothes as if they shrank from touch,
As if old, though not that yet, tired maybe,
And silent as two sullen absences,
Home late and neither noticing
How cold and dark the house had turned.

Both times her wing tightened to its peep-sight gray,
Mrs. Gilbert paused only briefly,
As though distracted by a name recalled,
Or stalled by something she'd misplaced;
Then, leaning ahead, the back wheels swiveled,
And as she moved her corridor returned to color.

The last room produces Mrs. Clement,
Who propped up in her partially raised bed
Is the best adjusted of them all;
Always with something gracious to say,
She thinks herself a guest in this hotel,
Where she appreciates the service
But occasionally asks for a different room.

With Mrs. Clement and all the rest settled,
And the bronze tinted windows darkening
Toward reflection, Mrs. Gilbert is free
To drive the few blocks home. Sometimes
She stops for something frozen, which she cooks

While listening to the news. After dinner
There are letters, the papers, the news again,
During which Mrs. Gilbert sometimes lists
The names of all the patients on her wing,
Now and for the last five years she's volunteered,
Feeling especially mindful of them now,
Between the two tall holidays,
With all the carols and the visits over
And for the next few quiet days
Little sense of anything ahead.

There's always the artificial tree to pack,
Practical because its needles do not drop,
It will not burn, requires no water,
Is light, and never changes size—
Its ornaments forever adequate . . .
And there are the clocks along the hall,
As round-faced and reassuring
As the watercolor seasons painted
On calendars some patients get by mail.

Limited and quirky as these comforts are,
Mrs. Gilbert finds them preferable
To the new clock radios the hospital
Has given as a present to each room,
All of them off-white, with digital faces
Blocked in crude illuminated reds
That reconfigure without changing place.
To Mrs. Gilbert, this collective gift,
A bargain no doubt, plays, in miniature,
All that Times Square, the hotel parties, Big Bands,
On the competing stations—all that these mean—
Summed up, she supposes, by the Times Square crowd itself.

Although she never waits till twelve,
Saying she cannot keep her eyelids up,
Mrs. Gilbert's not too sure how much she sleeps either,
Hearing in the white noise of the vent
Above her bed a rush of overlapping cries;
Only the air, but sometimes when she's tired
She remembers the man she heard about
Who claimed there was a way to play back sounds
Trapped like stilled echoes in rocks, the lava
Of Pompeii, say, the people in confusion,
Calling out and running to no escape.

And sometimes just before she's drifted off,
She hears the static of an old radio,
Her parents' Zenith, audible upstairs
Where she has waited in her bed, half asleep,
Holding out . . . first the background of the crowd,
Then suddenly all one voice and counting down,
As the last few seconds of the year
Widen like drained parentheses.

When she could not sleep without a light,
She too left her radio on for the voices;
She too wrote her husband short careful notes,
Placed beside a photograph or window,
A sentence or a phrase she hoped he'd catch,
Between all the folding and unfolding,
While at home, in bed, there were crosswords to do;
Propped up, her pillows banked a quiet minus,
As she piled their angles into height,
Wondering how deep a sleep could get
Drifting under a few half-completed words.
It was as if she stood dumb in her own name,

Or stilled before the plate glass to a shop
That, lights turned out, darkened and reflecting,
Gave her back a face she'd never seen.

But what she calls the taking down,
The season that she now walks through,
Stretches wide of any one reflection,
Wide even of her bringing water
To the few stalled days remaining
Of the shipped apples, oranges, and pears
Lining the complex sills to every room . . .
And the names, the essential names,
Answer through the hall's suffusing gray
As she feels somehow they always did,
Long before her leaning to the cart's odd wheels,
Or finding in the air's subtractive touch
That each was thirsty and completely recognized.

Poetry Titles in the Series

John Hollander, *"Blue Wine" and Other Poems*

Robert Pack, *Waking to My Name: New and Selected Poems*

Philip Dacey, *The Boy under the Bed*

Wyatt Prunty, *The Times Between*

Barry Spacks, *Spacks Street: New and Selected Poems*

Gibbons Ruark, *Keeping Company*

David St. John, *Hush*

Wyatt Prunty, *What Women Know, What Men Believe*

Adrien Stoutenberg, *Land of Superior Mirages: New and Selected Poems*

John Hollander, *In Time and Place*

Charles Martin, *Steal the Bacon*

John Bricuth, *The Heisenberg Variations*

Tom Disch, *Yes, Let's: New and Selected Poems*

Wyatt Prunty, *Balance as Belief*

Tom Disch, *Dark Verses and Light*

Thomas Carper, *Fiddle Lane*

Emily Grosholz, *Eden*

X. J. Kennedy, *Dark Horses*

Wyatt Prunty, *The Run of the House*

Designed by Martha Farlow

Composed by Blue Heron, Inc., in Adobe Caslon

Printed by Thomson-Shore, Inc., on 60-lb. Glatfelter Eggshell Cream